the Unspoken Words

PAIN, PATIENCE, AND PROGRESS

the Unspoken Words

PAIN, PATIENCE, AND PROGRESS

DANIELLE M. GILBERT

inkwell book co.

TABLE OF CONTENTS

TO MY MOTHER

My first best friend and nurturer. I'm forever grateful for your love and I dedicate this book to your life.

AND TO MY FAMILY

My husband Markie and my twin daughters Mariah and Makenzie; my drive, determination, and dedication comes from you.

INTRODUCTION

At a young age, I experienced the death of many loved ones. Within two years, I lost my baby boy, mother, cousin, great uncle, and grandfather. I often questioned God, not understanding why the people I love would leave me to this cruel world without a path to travel.

I often found myself in a dark room crying until I fell asleep, depressed, distant from friends, and lonely. There were many days I traveled different roads, cities, and places feeling hopeless.

But I knew the pain would not last forever, so I entered a phase of my life in which I devoted myself to learning how to be patient with God, myself, and life in general.

In order to understand how to walk the path God had ordered for me, I had to pray, read, listen, and walk in faith. My faith lead me to read a different quote, prayer, or poem every day. Before long I started to feel free and alive again. I felt the presence of my mother whispering in my ear, "Everything will be alright." I found comfort in her words every time I wanted to sit

The Unspoken Words

in the darkness to cry myself to sleep.

God reminded me, "Your pain will subside as you continue to believe in me." The days I felt like giving up, I read from a variety of authors, inspirational leaders, the Bible, or the internet, or sometimes simply listened to friends who encouraged me to be patient while I continue to be a work in progress.

The pain, patience, and progress I experienced have inspired me to share some of the daily quotes, poems, and prayers I utilized to embrace difficult life experiences, even (or perhaps especially) death. These are the words that provided me the strength, courage, and faith to continue on.

Danielle M. Gilbert, 2018

CHAPTER ONE

Pain

$\mathcal{P}$ain. Heartache. Frustration. Confusion. Loneliness. These emotions flowed through my body every second, minute, and hour of the day. Why did the man I loved harm my first-born child? He was only person I felt loved me, smiled at me, and was happy just to cuddle in my arms. Michael Leon Ross, my beautiful son, entered eternal life on September 26, 1997. I thought the pain would never end.

Oh, how I was so wrong—the pain continued. It was the word no family member ever wants to hear: cancer. My family learned that my mother had leukemia.

As a young child, I was confused by what cancer meant and how it could harm my precious mother. I continued with my life of going to school and hanging out with my girl friends. The doubt of my mother not making it through the pain never crossed my mind. She was a fighter—a woman who knew how to survive every obstacle that came her way.

The morning of May 28, 1998, the phone rang.

I answered, "Hello?"

     The Unspoken Words

"May I speak to Mr. Melvin Ross, the husband of Mrs. Ross?" said the voice on the other end.

"Sure, hold please."

An awkward silence entered the room. Minutes later came the words I never thought I'd hear: *your mother did not make it.* She did not make it out of the coma.

No way—not my mother. Pain. Heartache. Crying. I fell to the floor. Confusion. I felt lost. I was asking why.

These were the emotions that streamed through every bone in my body. The pain felt like a knife of devastation through the center of my heart.

Six months later, the pain remained as my uncle, aunt, and grandfather all entered eternal life also. Nightly, I fell to my knees, hands together, praying to the Heavenly Father to remove the sting of death which caused me so much pain...

Danielle Gilbert, author

We live in a society bloated with data yet starved for wisdom. We're connected 24/7, yet anxiety, fear, depression, and loneliness is at an all-time high.

We must course-correct.

Elizabeth Lindsey, explorer and ethnographer

May God bless you with discomfort at easy answers, half-truths, and superficial relationships, so that you may live deep within your heart.

May God bless you with anger at injustice, oppression, and exploitation of people, so that you may work for justice, freedom, and peace.

May God bless you with tears to shed for those who suffer pain, rejection, hunger, and war, so that you may reach out your hand to comfort them and turn their pain into joy.

And may God bless you with enough foolishness to believe that you can make a difference in the world, so that you can do what others claim cannot be done, to bring justice and kindness to all our children and the poor.

Franciscan Prayer

The Unspoken Words

For the Church, that she may continue to provide care and healing for all, especially those affected by the attacks on September 11, 2001, we pray to the Lord...

For all victims of violence and terrorism around the world, and for their families, that they may find comfort and peace, we pray to the Lord...

For the safety of our service men and women abroad, for civil servants who protect us and keep us safe, and for all who live with war and violence, we pray to the Lord...

For our leaders and for the leaders of nations, that they may work together to address the problems that provide fertile ground for the growth of terrorism, we pray to the Lord...

For the ability to forgive and for an end to all hatred, beginning in our own hearts, we pray to the Lord...

AMEN.

Prayer for September 11th

Lord, make me an instrument of your peace.
Where there is hatred, let me sow love;
Where there is injury, pardon;
Where there is doubt, faith;
Where there is despair, hope;
Where there is darkness, light;
Where there is sadness, joy;
O Divine Master, grant that I may not so much
    seek to be consoled, as to console;
To be understood, as to understand;
To be loved, as to love.
For it is in giving that we receive;
It is in pardoning that we are pardoned, and it is
    in dying that we are born to Eternal Life.

AMEN.

Peace Prayer of Saint Francis

Living God, creator of light, grant light to those who call upon you. Open our lips to praise you, our lives to proclaim your love, and our work to give you honor.

Author unknown

The Unspoken Words

Lord of hopefulness, awaken us. Show us the meaning in our labor, that we may ever rejoice in the promise of the seeds we sow.

Lord of righteousness, awaken us. Show us the good path, that we may walk in confidence in your wisdom and understanding.

Lord of hospitality, awaken us. Show us that our refuge is found in you, that we may always provide shelter to others in times of storm.

Catholic Relief Services

Wherever our most primal fears reside—our fears of the dark, of death, of being devoured, of meaninglessness, of lovelessness, or of loss—chances are good that beneath them lie gems of wisdom and maybe a vision or a calling.

Wherever you stumble—on a tree root, on a rock, on fear or shame, or vulnerability, on someone else's words, on the truth—dig there.

Gregg Levoy, Callings

Someone painted pictures on my
Windowpane last night—
Willow trees with trailing boughs
And flowers, frosty white,
And lovely crystal butterflies;
But when the morning sun
Touched them with its golden beams,
They vanished one by one.

Helen Bayley Davis poet

Dear God, if the light of joy is cast on the streets of my day, give me the courage to bask in it, and if possible, to dance.

AMEN.

Terry Hershey, minister and author

The ultimate measure of a person is not where one stands in moments of comfort and convenience, but where one stands at times of challenge and controversy.

Dr. Martin Luther King Jr., civil rights activist

Inspirer of my mind, consoler of my heart,
  healer of my spirit,
Thy presence lifts me from earth to heaven,
Thy words flow as the sacred river,
Thy thought rises as a divine spring,
Thy tender feelings waken sympathy in my heart.
Beloved Teacher, Thy very being is forgiveness.
The clouds of doubt and fear are scattered by
  Thy piercing glance.
All ignorance vanishes in Thy illuminating
  presence.
A new hope is born in my heart by breathing
  Thy peaceful atmosphere.
O inspiring Guide through life's puzzling ways,
  in Thee I feel abundance of blessing.

Sufi Prayer

Disturb us, Lord, when
We are too well pleased with ourselves,
When our dreams have come true
Because we have dreamed too little,
When we arrived safely
Because we sailed too close to the shore.
Disturb us, Lord, when

With the abundance of things we possess
We have lost our thirst
For the waters of life;
Having fallen in love with life,
We have ceased to dream of eternity
And in our efforts to build a new earth,
We have allowed our vision
Of the new Heaven to dim.
Disturb us, Lord, to dare more boldly,
To venture on wider seas
Where storms will show your mastery;
Where losing sight of land,
We shall find the stars.
We ask You to push back
The horizons of our hopes;
And to push into the future.
In strength, courage, hope, and love.

Commonly attributed to Sir Francis Drake

Normal day, let me be aware of the treasure you are. Let me learn from you, love you, bless you before you depart. Let me not pass you by in quest of some rare and perfect tomorrow. Let me hold you while I may, for it may not always be so.

 The Unspoken Words

One day I shall dig my nails into the earth, or
bury my face into the pillow, or stretch myself
taut, or raise my hands to the sky and want,
more than all the world, your return.

Mary Jean Iron, author

THE KNOTS PRAYER

Dear God, please untie the knots that are in my
mind, heart, and life.

Remove the have-knots, the can-knots, and
the do-knots that I have in my mind.

Erase the will-knots, may-knots, and might-
knots that may find a home in my heart.

Release me from the could-knots, would-
knots, and should-knots that obstruct my life.

Most of all, Father, I ask that you remove from
my mind, heart, and life all of the am-knots that
I have allowed to hold me back, and especially
the thought that I am not good enough.

Author unknown

Let the rain come and wash away the ancient
grudges, the bitter hatreds held and nurtured
over generations. Let the rain wash away the

memory of the hurt, the neglect.

Then let the sun come out and fill the sky with rainbows. Let the warmth of the sun heal us wherever we are broken.

Let it burn away the fog so that we can see each other clearly. So that we can see beyond labels, beyond accents, gender, or skin color.

Let the warmth and brightness of the sun melt our selfishness. So that we can share the joys and feel the sorrows of our neighbors.

And let the light of the sun be so strong that we will see all people as our neighbors.

Let the earth, nourished by rain, bring forth flowers to surround us with beauty.

And let the mountains teach our hearts to reach upward to heaven.

AMEN.

Rabbi Harold Kushner

*N*ever give up, for that is just the place and time that the tide will turn.

Harriet Beecher Stowe, author and abolitionist

   The Unspoken Words

Loneliness is the poverty of self; Solitude is the richness of self.

May Sarton, poet and novelist

Oh the comfort—the inexplicable comfort of feeling safe with a person—having neither to weigh thoughts nor measure words, but pouring them all right out, just as they are, chaff and grain together; certain that a faithful hand will take and sift them, keep what is worth keeping, and then with the breath of kindness blow the rest away.

Dina Maria Craik, A Life for a Life

Judging others makes us blind, whereas love is illuminating.

By judging others we blind ourselves to our own evil and to the grace which others are just as entitled to as we are.

Dietrich Bonhoeffer, The Cost of Discipleship

Growing spiritually can be like a roller coaster ride. Take comfort in the knowledge that the way down is only preparation for the way up.

Rebbe Nachman, founder of Breslov Hasidic movement

Every tomorrow has two handles. We can take hold of it with the handle of anxiety or the handle of faith.

Henry Ward Beecher, clergyman and social reformer

God of grace, you nurture us with a love deeper than any we know, and your will for us is always healing and salvation.

We praise and thank you, O God.

God of love, you enter into our lives, our pain, and our brokenness, and embrace us with your healing hands wherever we are.

We praise and thank you, O God.

God of strength, you fill us with your presence and send us forth with love and healing for all whom we meet.

We praise and thank you, O God.

AMEN.

Rev. Caroline Sproul Fairless, What Does Love Require?

Of all the forms of inequality, injustice in health is the most shocking and the most inhumane.

Dr. Martin Luther King Jr., civil rights activist

$\mathcal{T}$he basic order of life includes all the aspects of life—including those that are ugly and bitter and sad.

But even those qualities are part of the rich fabric of existence that can be woven into our being. In fact, we are already woven into that fabric whether we like it or not... We cannot change the way the world is, but by opening ourselves to the world as it is, we may find that gentleness, decency, and bravery are available— not only to us, but to all human beings.

Chögyam Trungpa, Buddhist meditation master

$\mathcal{T}$here is a light in this world, a healing spirit more powerful than any darkness we may encounter.

Saint Teresa of Calcutta

$\mathcal{I}$ sense that all is your creation and everything, and all of us, are being drawn back toward your loving heart.

Help me to be a person of peace, to speak about it in an uneasy world, and to live it among the people you have put into my life every day.

Light in me a desire to prepare for your

coming, to stand in the darkness waiting, eager
and filled with joy.

AMEN.

Author unknown

FEBRUARY TWILIGHT

I stood beside a hill
Smooth with new-laid snow,
A single star looked out
From the cold evening glow.
There was no other creature
That saw what I could see—
I stood and watched the evening star
As long as it watched me.

Sara Teasdale, poet

CAREGIVER'S PRAYER

*H*ere I am, Lord
I seek your vision and strength
I call upon your steadfast love.
For you are with me in my desire
to care for and comfort your people.
Open my eyes to see sorrow.
Open my ears to hear distress.

    The Unspoken Words

Open my heart to love patiently.
Open my lips to speak kindly.
Walk with me, Lord, and guide me.
Renew my spirit and bless my work.
Strengthen me to care for the ill.
Inspire me to see new horizons.
Fill my heart with hope.
You have heard my prayer.

Sandra Lucas, chaplain

For many of us, the waters of our daily life are anything but calm because we don't create conscious space for intentional breathing or silence as part of our daily experience... When we pause and breathe consciously, we open the portal to the Presence and enter a sacred silence where the waters are always calm.

Dennis Merritt Jones, The Art of Uncertainty

Here I stand. I can do no other. God help me.

AMEN.

Martin Luther, Protestant reformer

*U*ncertainty is the only certainty there is, and knowing how to live with insecurity is the only security.

Professor John Allen Paulos, author

PRAYING

*I*t doesn't have to be
the blue iris, it could be
weeds in a vacant lot, or a few
small stones; just
pay attention, then patch
a few words together and don't try
to make them elaborate, this isn't
a contest but the doorway
into thanks, and a silence in which
another voice may speak.

Mary Oliver, poet

NATIONAL PRAYER FOR PEACE

*A*lmighty God, Who has given us this good land for our heritage; We humbly beseech thee that we may always prove ourselves a people mindful of Thy favor and glad to do thy will. Bless our

     The Unspoken Words

land with honorable ministry, sound learning, and pure manners.

Save us from violence, discord, and confusion, from pride and arrogance, and from every evil way. Defend our liberties, and fashion into one united people, the multitude brought hither out of many kindreds and tongues. Endow with Thy spirit of wisdom those whom in Thy name we entrust the authority of government, that there may be justice and peace at home, and that through obedience to Thy law, we may show forth thy praise among the nations of the earth. In time of prosperity fill our hearts with thankfulness, and in the day of trouble, suffer not our trust in Thee to fail; all of which we ask through Jesus Christ our Lord.

AMEN.

Author unknown, *1928 Book of Common Prayer*

Fasting is the soul of prayer, mercy is the lifeblood of fasting. If we have not all three together, we have nothing.

Saint Peter Chrysologus

Laundry is the only thing that should be separated by color.

Author unknown

Let there be peace, welfare and righteousness
in every part of the world.
Let confidence and friendship prevail
for the good of east and west...
for the good of all humanity.
Let the people inspire their leaders
helping them to seek peace by peaceful means
helping them and urging them
to build a better world
a world with a home for everybody
a world with food and work for everybody
a world with spiritual freedom
for everybody...
Let those who have power
deal respectfully with the resources of the planet.
Let them respect and maintain
the purity of the air, water, land and subsoil...
Let ordinary people
meet by the millions across the borders...
Let billions of human beings

The Unspoken Words

co-operate to create a good future
for their children and grandchildren...

Hagan Hasselbalch, film director

*Y*our ways, O Lord, make known to me; teach me your paths, guide me in your truth and teach me.

Psalm 25:4-5

*D*o not be depressed. Do not let your weakness make you impatient. Instead, let the serenity of your spirit shine through your face. Let the joy of your mind burst forth. Let words of thanks break from your lips.

Saint Peter Damian

*P*rotect me, God,
Because I come to you for safety.
I say "You are my God;
All good things I have come from you."
How wonderful are your faithful people!
My greatest pleasure is to be with them.

Psalm 16

Where the mind is without fear and the head is
    held high,
Where knowledge is free,
Where the world has not been broken up into
    fragments,
By narrow domestic walls,
Where words come out from the depth of truth,
Where tireless striving stretches its arms towards
    perfection,
Where the clear stream of reason has not lost its way,
Into the dreary desert sand of dead habit,
Where the mind is led forward,
Into ever-widening thought and action,
Into that heaven of freedom, let my world awake.

Rabindranath Tagore, poet

If we accept and acquiesce in the face of
discrimination, we accept the responsibility
ourselves and allow those responsible to salve
their conscience by believing that they have
our acceptance and concurrence. We should,
therefore, protest openly everything... that
smacks of discrimination or slander.

Mary McLeod Bethune, educator, author, civil rights activist

    The Unspoken Words

What actions are
most excellent?
To gladden the heart
Of a human being.
To feed the hungry.
To help the afflicted.
To lighten the sorrow
of the sorrowful.
To remove the wrongs
of the injured.
That person is the
beloved of God
who does good
to God's creatures.

The Prophet Muhammad

You suppose you are the trouble
But you are the cure
You suppose that you are the lock on the door
But you are the key that opens it
It's too bad that you want to be someone else
You don't see your own face, your own beauty
Yet, no face is more beautiful than yours.

Rumi, poet

Grant me the ability to be alone;
May it be my custom to go outdoors each day
Among the trees and grasses,
Among the growing things,
And there I may be alone,
To talk with the one that I belong to.

Rebbe Nachman, founder of Breslov Hasidic movement

Make me, Lord
Obedient without complaint
Poor without regret
Patient without murmur
Humble without pretense
Joyful without foolishness
Truthful without disguise

Saint Thomas Aquinas

May the road rise to meet you.
May the wind be always at your back.
May the sun shine warm upon your face;
The rains fall soft upon your fields
And, until we meet again,
May God hold you in the palm of His hand.

A Gaelic Blessing

A PRAYER FOR BLESSED ACCEPTANCE

Dear God, in this moment I hold your acceptance. You love me completely, just as I am. You see my great potential within, and you nurture my tender heart of compassion.

In this moment, I let your acceptance be my own. I accept others as the children of God. I hold high their inner greatness, always seeking to serve the highest and best within all people. And so it is.

Vicky Thompson, Journey to Spiritual Awakening

PRECIOUS IN GOD'S SIGHT

Precious in God's sight you are,
Divinely made in God's delight,
Endowed with beauty wove deep within,
Brighter than the darkest sin.
Free in God's sight you are,
To rise in rainbow'd glory.
To claim the God-light in your soul
And tell the world your story.

Edwina Gateley, A Mystical Heart

There are no ordinary people. You have never talked to a mere mortal. Nations, cultures, arts, civilizations – these are mortal, and their life is to ours as the life of a gnat. But it is immortals whom we joke with, work with, marry, snub, and exploit – immortal horrors or everlasting splendors. This does not mean that we are to be perpetually solemn. We must play. But our merriment must be of that kind (and it is, in fact, the merriest kind) which exists between people who have, from the outset, taken each other seriously – no flippancy, no superiority, no presumption.

C.S. Lewis, The Weight of Glory

If I spent enough time with the tiniest creature—even a caterpillar—I would never have to prepare a sermon. So full of God is every creature.

Meister Eckhart, theologian and philosopher

$\mathcal{O}$ Lord, to you I call; hasten to me;
hearken to my voice when I call upon you.
Let my prayer come like incense before you;
the lifting up of my hands,
like the evening sacrifice.

Psalm 141:1-2, adapted

$\mathcal{W}$e are not human beings having a spiritual experience. We are spiritual beings having a human experience.

Pierre Teilhard de Chardin, Jesuit priest and philosopher

$\mathcal{E}$veryone has a sanctuary, if only in the mind. Even if we can't say what it is, we know of its power. It is a place where we feel grounded, unhurried, and renewed.

Terry Hershey, *Sanctuary*

$\mathcal{H}$appiness can only be achieved by looking inward and learning to enjoy whatever life has, and this requires transforming greed into gratitude.

Saint John Chrysostom

Missal of Pope Pius V

WE PLOUGH THE FIELDS AND SCATTER

We plough the fields and scatter
The good seed on the land,
But it is fed and watered
By God's almighty hand;
God sends the snow in winter,
The warmth to swell the grain,
The breezes and the sunshine,
And soft refreshing rain:
All good gifts around us,
Are sent from heav'n above,
Then thank the Lord, O thank the Lord
For such great love.

Matthius Claudius, poet and journalist

The Unspoken Words

If you have never walked a day in my shoes, why do you judge the way you do?

Have you felt like you were never good enough?

Have you ever felt lost wondering, who would love you then learn it was the wrong love?

Have you wanted a true love aka a father figure then learn booze was his true love?

Have you ever watched a dove fly over your only best friend, your mother?

Have you ever just wanted to hear the words of your mother over and over and over again, you listened it was dead silence?

Have you ever kneed to the ground asking *God why me? Why would you take my child, father, mother, grandfather, aunt and uncle?*

Where do I go from here?

God are you here, here to protect me?

If you never walked a day in my shoes why do you judge me the way that you do?

Danielle Gilbert, author

The Unspoken Words

NOTES

NOTES

The Unspoken Words

NOTES

CHAPTER TWO

Patience

Patience. I never understood how to be patient with life—most importantly with God's plan for me. Through the pain of death, getting to know myself, and prayer, I never thought God was preparing me for the destiny He designed especially for me.

Some days, patience came a lot harder for me than others. Day after day I prayed but with no response. I asked, *why are my prayers falling on deaf ears?* Why wouldn't God move me into a place of happiness? Sitting on the edge of my bed on a Sunday afternoon, I prayed that the Spirit fill me, empower me, and direct me as I waited on the Lord. I have to admit; the silence was slowly killing me inside.

The New Bible Dictionary defines patience as "God-given restraint in the face of opposition or oppression." My role was to trust the Holy Spirit to provide the strength to hold on, and then act accordingly to my faith in that promise.

I did just that—my spirit lead me to Galatians 5:22-26 (New International Version (NIV)). According to Galatians 5, patience is often called longsuffering. I saw patience as a God-

The Unspoken Words

given restraint—it was my choice to accept it and act in intentional obedience.

The process of obedience led me to reading Hebrews 12:2. That scripture clarified that Christ's death and life is the reason we can be filled with, and empowered by, the Holy Spirit. My trials and obstacles lead me to expand my faith to become more close with God and relay on him more intentionally. In scripture, James 1:2-4 tells us it is here that a mature and complete faith is grown. My faith has grown enormously.

I stood firm in my faith knowing God would eradicate the pain. Patience is an act of the determination to claim a path for the Kingdom of God, and it is rewarded richly by Him. Revelation 3:10-11 tells us of God's care for those who persevere through the battle. I'm now walking in my purpose with God's armor around me.

Danielle Gilbert, author

Lord, it is night.
The night is for stillness.
Let us be still in the presence of God.
It is night after a long day.
What has been done has been done;
What has not been done has not been done;
  let it be.
The night is dark.
Let our fears of the darkness of the world and of
  our own lives rest in you.
The night is quiet.
Let the quietness of your peace enfold us, all
  dear to us, and all who have no peace.
The night heralds the dawn.
Let us look expectantly to a new day, new joys,
  new possibilities.
In your name we pray.

AMEN.

New Zealand Prayer Book

How lovely to think that no one need wait a moment, we can start now, start slowly changing the world! How lovely that everyone, great and small, can make their contribution toward

The Unspoken Words

introducing justice straightaway... And you can always, always give something, even if it is only kindness!

Anne Frank, *The Diary of a Young Girl*

Because I remember, I despair. Because I remember, I have the duty to reject despair.

Elie Wiesel, "Hope, Despair, and Memory"

Lord,
How silently,
How silently
The wondrous gift is given.
I would be silent now,
Lord,
And expectant. . .
That I may receive
The gift I need,
So I may become the gifts others need.

AMEN.

Ted Loder, *Guerillas of Grace*

May today there be peace within. May you trust God that you are exactly where you are meant to be. May you not forget the infinite possibilities that are born of faith.

May you use those gifts that you have received, and pass on the love that has been given to you. May you be confident knowing you are a child of God.

Let this presence settle into your bones, and allow your soul the freedom to sing, dance, praise and love. It is there for each and every one of us.

Saint Teresa of Ávila

O Thou kind Lord! Unite all. Let the religions agree and make the nations one, so that they may see each other as one family and the whole earth as one home. May they all live together in perfect harmony. Raise aloft the banner of the oneness of humankind.

O God! Establish the Most Great Peace.

Cement Thou, O God, the hearts together.

O Thou kind Parent, God! Gladden our hearts through the fragrance of Thy love. Brighten our eyes through the Light of Thy Guidance.

The Unspoken Words

Delight our ears with the melody of Thy Word, and shelter us all in the Stronghold of Thy Providence.

Thou art the Mighty and Powerful, Thou art the Forgiving and Thou art the One Who overlooketh the shortcomings of all humankind.

'Abdu'l-Bahá', Bahá'í Faith Leader

O God,
Who makes all things new,
new stars, new dust, new life,
take my heart, every hardened
edge and measured beat, and
create something new in me.
I need your newness, God, the
rough parts of me made
smooth; the stagnant stirred;
the stuck freed; the unkind
forgiven. And then, by the
power of Your Spirit, I need to
be turned toward Love again.

AMEN.

Pamela C. Hawkins, The Awkward Season

Humility is not thinking less of yourself, it's thinking of yourself less.

Rick Warren, The Purpose Driven Life

People travel to wonder at the height of mountains, at the huge waves of the sea, at the long courses of rivers, at the vast compass of the ocean, at the circular motion of the stars; and they pass by themselves without wondering... Now, let us acknowledge the wonder of our physical incarnation—that we are here, in these particular bodies, at this particular time, in these particular circumstances. May we never take for granted the gift of our individuality.

Saint Augustine of Hippo, The Confessions of St. Augustine

You can find energizing moments in each aspect of your life, but to do so you must learn how to catch them... and allow yourself to follow where they lead.

Marcus Buckingham, Find Your Strongest Life

Keep my words,
and treasure my commands.
Keep my commands and live,
my teaching as the apple of your eye;
Bind them on your fingers,
write them on the tablet of your heart.
Say to Wisdom, "You are my sister!"
call Understanding, "Friend!"

Proverbs 7:1-4

Mindfully practicing authenticity during our most soul-searching struggles is how we invite grace, joy, and gratitude into our lives.

Brené Brown, *The Gifts of Imperfection*

A WINTER PRAYER

Let us huddle together this morning, our community a place of warmth in our lives as we share the flame of hope and connection.

Let us allow the frost of isolation and bitterness to melt away as we open ourselves to a sense of peace and spirit.

We extend our thoughts to all those who are cold this morning, lacking shelter or love to keep them warm.

Let us wrap our prayers around them and each other like scarves, and wish each other safe journeys through the storm.

May we be insulated from fear as the earth is insulated by the snow, and, like bulbs, may we continue to grow and open inside, despite the cold, ready for the spring, to stretch and grow towards justice.

AMEN.
Rev. Kate Wilkinson

The word 'listen' contains the same letters as the word 'silent.'

Alfred Brendel, pianist

To yield is to be preserved whole.
To be bent is to become straight
To be empty is to be full.
To be worn out is to be renewed.
To have little is to possess.
To have plenty is to be perplexed.
Therefore the sage embraces the One
And becomes the model of the world.

   The Unspoken Words

He does not show himself; therefore he is
    luminous.
She does not justify herself; therefore she
    becomes prominent.
He does not boast of himself; therefore he is
    given credit.
She does not brag; therefore she can endure for
    long.
It is precisely because he does not compete that
    the world cannot compete with him.

Lau Tzu, Tao Te Ching

*G*od of all goodness, grant us to desire ardently,
to seek wisely, to know surely, and to accomplish
perfectly Thy holy will, for the glory of Thy
name.

Saint Thomas Aquinas

**Take into account that great love
and great achievements involve
great risk.**

Jackson Brown and H. Jackson Brown, Jr.

Life's Little Instruction Book

I have learned over the years that when one's mind is made up, this diminishes fear.

Rosa Parks, civil rights activist

*W*herever you turn your eyes, the world can shine like transfiguration. You don't have to bring a thing to it except a little willingness to see.

Marilynne Robinson, *Gilead*

Blessed is the one who has concern for the poor.

Psalm 41:2

*L*ove is patient, love is kind. It is not jealous, love is not pompous, it is not inflated, it is not rude, it does not seek its own interests, it is not quick tempered, it does not brood over injury, it does not rejoice over wrongdoing but rejoices with the truth. It bears all things, believes all things, hopes all things, endures all things.

1 Corinthians 13:4-7

  The Unspoken Words

God of peace, thank you for a society that honors the achievements and sacrifices of all people.

This February, bless all who, in the spirit of Black History Month, seek to bring your world together with love and compassion.

Bless all your beloved children, Loving God, and teach us to live together in peace, now and always.

AMEN.

Author unknown

I've learned from experience that the greater part of our happiness or misery depends on our dispositions and not on our circumstances.

Martha Washington, "Letter to Mercy Warren"

What God intended for you goes far beyond anything you can imagine.

Oprah Winfrey, media mogul and philanthropist

Holy Spirit of Wisdom,
You refresh us with your life-saving power.
You have entrusted us with a share in leadership.
Help us to share ideas and plans with each other.

Keep us kind and courteous to one another.
Give us insight to the work at hand
that we may further your causes and benefit
   many people.
Help us to resist any temptation to dominate,
control or forget the needs of all.
We ask this in your holy name.

AMEN.

Author unknown

Bless all who worship you, almighty God,
from the rising of the sun to its setting:
from your goodness enrich us,
by your love inspire us,
by your Spirit guide us,
by your power protect us,
in your mercy receive us,
now and always.

Author unknown

Our Father, who hast set a restlessness in our
hearts, and made us all seekers after that which
we can never fully find; forbid us to be satisfied
with what we make of life.

     The Unspoken Words

Draw us from base content, and set our eyes on far-off goals. Keep us at tasks too hard for us, that we may be driven to Thee for strength. Deliver us from fretfulness and self-pity; make us sure of the good we cannot see, and of the hidden good in the world. Open our eyes to simple beauty all around us, and our hearts to the loveliness men hide from us because we do not try enough to understand them. Save us from ourselves, and show us a vision of a world made new. May Thy spirit of peace and illumination so enlighten our minds that all life shall glow with new meaning and new purpose...

Eleanor Roosevelt, diplomat and former First Lady

Life is like a camera:
Just focus on what's
Important and capture
the good times,
develop from the
negatives, and if things
don't work out, just
take another shot.

Author unknown

Stand fast, therefore, in this conduct: firm and unchangeable in faith, loving each other, united in truth...

Saint Polycarp, "Letter to the Philippians"

In order to cooperate with life we must learn how to forgive, how to pray, how to receive, how to adjust....

Seeking nothing, giving everything, loving all people, trusting God...loving each moment fully.

Author unknown

The higher goal of spiritual living is not to amass a wealth of information, but to face sacred moments.

Rabbi Abraham Heschel

Never let a problem to be solved become more important than a person to be loved.

Thomas S. Monson, "Finding Joy in the Journey"

*I*f I do not believe, if I do not make what is called an act of faith, if I did not have faith that the works of mercy do lighten the sum total of suffering in the world, so that those who are suffering in this ghastly struggle somehow mysteriously find their pain lifted and some balm of consolation poured on their wounds, if I did not believe in these things, the problem of evil would indeed be overwhelming.

Dorothy Day, On Pilgrimage

*W*hat lies behind you and what lies in front of you, pales in comparison to what lies inside of you.

Ralph Waldo Emerson, writer and poet

*I*f all the things I have done,
all the love I have given,
all the panels I have nailed to walls,
all the words I have written,
if they would all disappear –
God would still be present,
and God would still love me,
for our God is a faithful God.

Paula Pearce, Prayers from Franciscan Hearts, adapted

$\mathcal{T}$o the Creator of nature and man, of truth and beauty, I pray:

Hear my voice, for it is the voice of the victims of all wars and violence among individuals and nations.

Hear my voice, for it is the voice of all children who suffer and will suffer when people put their faith in weapons and war.

Hear my voice when I beg You to instill into the hearts of all human beings the wisdom of peace, the strength of justice, and the joy of fellowship.

Hear my voice, for I speak for the multitudes in every country and in every period of history who do not want war and are ready to walk the road of peace.

Hear my voice and grant insight and strength so that we may always respond to hatred with love, to injustice with total dedication to justice, to need with the sharing of self, to war with peace.

O God, hear my voice and grant unto the world Your everlasting peace.

Pope John Paul II, L'Osservatore Romano, 3-9-81,14

     The Unspoken Words

*H*ope is not the expectation that things will be better tomorrow; hope is the capacity to do the right thing today.

Mitri Raheb, Lutheran pastor

*L*oving God,

I pray for courage as I begin this day, for I understand there is work to be done, burdens to be carried, feelings to be shared, and joys to be celebrated.

Grant me the courage to be silent, that I may hear your voice; to persevere, that I may share your life; and to remember, lest I forget the way by which you have led me.

And when this day is done, Loving God, may I have the courage to see your guiding hand in the friendships that have been made, in the hurts that have been healed, and in the strength that has been given.

AMEN.

Author unknown

O God, we commit ourselves to be your loving hands.

Bless and guide the hands and minds of those who work in the ministry of healthcare.

Bless all who work in hospitals and nursing homes, and places in which care is offered. Through their efforts may your healing power restore health and peace, hope and strength.

Grant them all the skill and wisdom and love to do your healing work.

O God, we commit ourselves to be your loving hands.

John F. Wallenhorst

No task, rightly done, is truly private. It is part of the world's work.

President Woodrow Wilson

Lead us from death to life,
from falsehood to truth.
Lead us from despair to hope,
from fear to trust.
Let peace fill our hearts,
our world, our universe.

Let us dream together,
pray together,
work together,
to build one world
of peace and justice for all.

Author unknown, A New Zealand Prayer Book

Grant me the grace to spend this day without offending you and without failing my neighbor.

Saint Louise de Marillac

The truth knocks on the door and you say, "Go away. I'm looking for the truth," and so it goes away. Puzzling.

Robert Pirsig, Zen and the Art of Motorcycle Maintenance

Spirit of love and life, be with us in these moments as we gather to do the business of the day.

May we remember to listen well, and speak clearly, may we be present to one another here in this time as we are in worship.

And gathering to do the business of this ministry, let us always remember its work: to find the lost, to mend what is broken, to offer a word of healing where there is pain and trouble, to speak into the world a word of hope and of peace a word of justice into a world so in need and always to speak an alleluia for life in its glory and grace, an alleluia for life in its worry and trouble, alleluia for all.

Rev. Dr. Linda Hart, adapted

May today there be peace within.

May you trust God that you are exactly where you are meant to be.

May you not forget the infinite possibilities that are born of faith.

May you use those gifts that you have received, and pass on the love that has been given to you.

May you be confident knowing you are a child of God.

Let this presence settle into your bones, and allow your soul the freedom to sing, dance, praise and love.

It is there for each and every one of us.

Saint Teresa of Ávila

*H*oly One,
You who gives
Strength to each
one of us in times
of trial, we pray
for those today
who struggle
to have their
voices heard.
May we all seek
steadfast courage
to stand up for
justice, lending
our support in
defense of those
in our world who
cannot defend
themselves.

AMEN.

Author unknown

Go like the wind, which has its start at the center of things but has no end, as life does not. Life has within it movement and purpose. This movement is unceasing, this purpose unyielding. Go. Go like the wind.

AMEN.

L. Annie Foerster, *For Praying Out Loud*

God help us live slowly
To move simply
To look softly
To allow emptiness
To let the heart create for us.

AMEN.

Michael Leunig, cartoonist

None of us got where we are solely by pulling ourselves up by our bootstraps.

We got here because somebody—a parent, a teacher, an Ivy League crony or a few nuns—bent down and helped us pick up our boots.

Thurgood Marshall, Supreme Court Justice

$\mathcal{T}$here must be a time when we cease speaking to be fully present with ourselves.

There must be a time when we exclude clamor by listening to nothing whatsoever.

There must be a time when we forgo our plans as if we had no plans at all.

There must be a time when we abandon conceits and tap into a deeper wisdom.

There must be a time when we stop striving and find the peace within.

AMEN.

David O. Rankin, minister and author

$\mathcal{I}$ now place a higher value on this self-permission to relax and release my mind from constantly thinking about commitments and obligations.

This freedom opens me up to be more present to the people....

Essentially, it is a freedom to notice God's presence in my life...to the realness of life.

Nicole Campion

NOTES

The Unspoken Words

NOTES

The Unspoken Words

NOTES

NOTES

CHAPTER THREE

Progress

Progress. Onward movement towards the destination of progress finally set in ten years later. The emotions of loss are arguably the most unique and confusing feelings with which to cope. Managing with immediate feelings of loss, as well as the difficult emotions that can persist over time, led me to journal my thoughts.

Crying and kneeling became a daily routine. Laying in the bed, looking to the ceiling, asking, *Why? Why me, Lord? What did I do, Lord, for You to take my loved ones away? I need You to help me progress through these steps of grief. I want to be healed.*

But whenever I took one step forward I seemed to then take two steps backward. My confusion led me to a state of depression—a mental illness no one wants to be diagnosed with.

The signs of progress were difficult to realize. Daily, I found a poem or quotation to guide me through the pain of death, but I needed help.

The following year, progress started. It started with realization of being in touch with the finality of the death. I finally knew my love ones were not coming back; however, they had

The Unspoken Words

entered the gates of eternal life. They will never return to earth, but their memories can live on.

The pleasant (and unpleasant) memories ran through my mind day after day. Memories that became painful as they reminded me of how much I had lost. I looked to my family and friends to share the pleasant memories of our loved ones instead.

Driving and crying was no longer my normal. It was the best sensation when I could drive without crying once the entire time. I looked forward to the holidays again. I could sit through a church service without crying. I even had enough patience with myself to cope through "grief attacks." I knew they were becoming further apart, less frightening, and less painful.

This is what I call progress.

Danielle Gilbert, author

LIFE

Life is an opportunity, benefit from it.
Life is beauty, admire it.
Life is bliss, taste it.
Life is a dream, realize it.
Life is a challenge, meet it.
Life is a duty, complete it.
Life is a game, play it.
Life is costly, care for it.
Life is wealth, keep it.
Life is love, enjoy it.
Life is mystery, know it.
Life is a promise, fulfill it.
Life is sorrow, overcome it.
Life is a song, sing it.
Life is a struggle, accept it.
Life is tragedy, confront it.
Life is an adventure, dare it.
Life is luck, make it.
Life is too precious, do not destroy it.
Life is life, fight for it.

Saint Teresa of Calcutta

Loving God, we offer you,
Every flower that ever grew,
Every bird that ever flew,
Every wind that ever blew,
Every thunder rolling,
Every church bell tolling,
Every leaf and sod,
Every wave that ever moved,
Every heart that ever loved,
Every river dashing,
Every cloud that swept o'er the skies,
Every human joy and woe,
Watch over us today as we strive,
to understand your word of love.

AMEN.

Irish prayer, adapted

Creator God, mighty worker, humble servant,

We offer prayers for our sisters and brothers who minister with us.

As our labor serves others by providing loving service, may it also serve you in its diligence, dignity, and justice.

May we all be guided by the common good,

not self-interest.

May justice rule over profit.

May safety reign over risk.

May love overwhelm harsh rules.

Bless us all, living God, and raise up our co-workers, glad to labor in your name, and striving together to build your Beloved Community.

AMEN.

Author unknown

NEW YEAR'S PRAYER

Thank you Lord for giving me
The brand new year ahead
Help me live the way I should
As each new day I tread.
Give me gentle wisdom
That I might help a friend
Give me strength and courage
So a shoulder I might lend.
The year ahead is empty
Help me fill it with good things
Each new day filled with joy
And the happiness it brings.
Please give the leaders of our world

The Unspoken Words

A courage born of peace
That they might lead us gently
And all the fighting cease.
Please give to all upon this earth
A heart that's filled with love
A gentle happy way to live
With Your blessings from above.

Charlotte Anselmo

*J*oy does not
simply happen
to us. We have to
choose joy and
keep choosing it
every day.

Henri J.M. Nouwen, Dutch priest, professor, and writer

*P*rayer is an attitude toward life that sees
everything as ultimately sacred,
everything as potentially life-changing,
everything as revelatory of life's meaning.
It is our link between dailiness and eternity.

Joan Chittister, Benedictine nun and author

People are like stained-glass windows. They sparkle and shine when the sun is out, but when the darkness sets in, their true beauty is revealed only if there is a light from within.

Elisabeth Kübler-Ross, psychiatrist

The ones who are crazy enough to think they can change the world, are the ones who do.

Steve Jobs, entrepreneur

To listen is very hard, because it asks of us so much interior stability that we no longer need to prove ourselves by speeches, arguments, statements or declarations. True listeners no longer have an inner need to make their presence known. They are free to receive, to welcome, to accept.

Listening is much more than allowing another to talk while waiting for a chance to respond. Listening is paying full attention to others and welcoming them into our very beings. The beauty of listening is that those who are listened to start feeling accepted, start taking their words

The Unspoken Words

more seriously and discovering their true selves. Listening is a form of spiritual hospitality by which you invite strangers to become friends, to get to know their inner selves more fully, and even to dare to be silent with you.

Henri J.M. Nouwen, *Bread for the Journey*

A friend is one that knows you as you are, understands where you have been, accepts what you have become, and still, gently allows you to grow.

Author unknown

We make a living by what we get, but we make a life by what we give.

Author unknown

TO A CHILD DANCING IN THE WIND
*D*ance there upon the shore;
What need have you to care
For wind or water's roar?
And tumble out your hair

That the salt drops have wet;
Being young you have not known
The fool's triumph, nor yet
Love lost as soon as won,
Nor the best labourer dead
And all the sheaves to bind.
What need have you to dread
The monstrous crying of wind?

W.B. Yeats, Responsibilities and Other Poems

*B*ecause of your smile, you make life more beautiful.

Thich Nhat Hanh, Buddhist monk

*B*less our hearts, God, with light and love
that we may bring your word of compassion,
and be a sign of liberation for all.

Author unknown

*E*very great dream begins with a dreamer.
Always remember, you have within you
the strength, the patience, and the passion
to reach for the stars to change the world.

Commonly attributed to Harriet Tubman

Keep your thoughts positive because your thoughts become your words.

Keep your words positive because your words become your behavior.

Keep your behavior positive because your behavior becomes your habits.

Keep your habits positive because your habits become your values.

Keep your values positive because your values become your destiny.

Mahatma Gandhi, Indian political and spiritual leader

Listen to your heart. Because wherever your heart is, that is where you'll find your treasure.

Paulo Coelho, *The Alchemist*

Do good while you still have time.

Commonly attributed to Saint John Bosco

Kindness is the language the blind can see and the deaf can hear.

Author unknown

It is about making the choice:
To be open.
To be available.
To be curious.
To be alive.
To be willing to be surprised by joy.

Terry Hershey, *Sanctuary*

With malice toward none; with charity for all; with firmness in the right, as God gives us to see the right, let us strive on to finish the work we are in; to bind up the nation's wounds... to do all which may achieve and cherish a just and lasting peace among ourselves and with all nations.

Abraham Lincoln, "The Second Inaugural Address"

Each person must live their life as a model for others.

Rosa Parks, civil rights activist

There is an appointed time for everything, and a time for every affair under the heavens.

A time to be born, and a time to die; a time to plant, and a time to uproot the plant.

A time to kill, and a time to heal; a time to tear down, and a time to build.

A time to weep, and a time to laugh; a time to mourn, and a time to dance.

A time to scatter stones, and a time to gather them; a time to embrace, and a time to be far from embraces.

A time to seek, and a time to lose; a time to keep, and a time to cast away.

A time to rend, and a time to sew; a time to be silent, and a time to speak.

A time of love, and a time to hate;

A time of war, and a time of peace.

Ecclesiastes 3:1-8

Devote yourselves to prayer, keeping alert in it with thanksgiving.

Colossians 4:2

We don't stop playing because we grow old; We grow old because we stop playing.

Author unknown

BE AT PEACE

Do not fear the changes of life—
Rather look to them with full hope as they arise.
God, whose very own you are,
Will deliver you from out of them.
God has kept you hitherto,
And God will lead you safely through all things;
And when you cannot stand it,
God will wrap you in love.
Do not be afraid of what may happen tomorrow;
The same everlasting God who cares for you
   today
Will take care of you then and every day.
God will either shield you from suffering,
Or God will give you unfailing strength to bear it.
Be at Peace—
And put aside all anxious thoughts and
   imaginations.

Saint Francis de Sales

The nicest place to be is in someone's thoughts!
The safest place to be is in someone's prayers!
And the best place to be is in God's hands!

Author unknown

THE OPTIMIST'S CREED

*P*romise Yourself...

To be so strong that nothing can disturb your peace of mind.

To talk health, happiness, and prosperity to every person you meet.

To make all your friends feel that there is something in them.

To look at the sunny side of everything and make your optimism come true.

To think only the best, to work only for the best, and to expect only the best.

To be just as enthusiastic about the success of others as you are about your own.

To forget the mistakes of the past and press on to the greater achievements of the future.

To wear a cheerful countenance at all times and give every living creature you meet a smile.

To give so much time to the improvement of yourself that you have no time to criticize others.

To be too large for worry, too noble for anger, too strong for fear, and too happy to permit the presence of trouble.

Christian D. Larson, The Optimist Creed

One new perception,
one fresh thought,
one act of surrender,
one change of heart,
one leap of faith,
can change your life forever.

Robert Holden, psychologist and author

PRAYER FOR INTERNATIONAL WOMEN'S DAY

Women are a reflection of the glory of God. Today we honor the women of all times and all places:

Women of courage.

Women of hope.

Women suffering

Women mourning.

Women living fully.

Women experiencing joy.

Women delighting in life.

Women knowing the interconnectedness of the human family.

Women honoring the sacredness of the relational, the affective.

The Unspoken Words

Women quietly tending the garden of human flourishing.

Women boldly leading the transformation of unjust global structures.

Women seeking Wisdom.

Women sharing Wisdom.

Women receiving Love.

Women giving Love.

Women: life-giving.

Women: the image of God.

Loving God, we celebrate your faithfulness and love. On this day we commit ourselves to the promotion of the full humanity of all women everywhere. We know that whatever denies, diminishes, or distorts the full humanity of women is not of God.

Help us to be faithful to your call.

Education for Justice

"It's impossible," said pride. "It's risky," said experience. "It's pointless," said reason. "Give it a try," whispered the heart.

Author unknown

Say goodbye to the past.
List the things/feelings I'm letting go of.
Today, I want to feel grateful, at peace, inspired
and productive.

Author unknown

May I become at all times, both now and
forever,
A protector for those without protection
A guide for those who have lost their way
A ship for those with oceans to cross
A sanctuary for those in danger
A lamp for those without light
A place of refuge for those who lack shelter
And a servant to all in need.

Traditional Buddhist prayer

The secret of creating peace is that when you
listen to other people you have only one purpose:
to offer them an opportunity to open their hearts.
If you can keep that awareness and compassion
alive in you, then you can sit and listen for an
hour even if the other person expresses wrong

   The Unspoken Words

perceptions, condemnation, and bitterness. You can continue to listen because you are protected by the nectar of compassion in your own heart. Keeping your awareness keeps you safe in your own peace.

Thich Nhat Hanh, Buddhist monk

PRAYER TO SAINT JOSEPH

You are the patron of families; do not let those who have children to support and raise lack the necessary means. Have pity on our brothers and sisters held down in unemployment and poverty because of sickness or social disorders. Help our political leaders and captains of industry find new and just solutions. May each and every one have the joy of contributing, according to his abilities, to the common prosperity by an honorable livelihood. Grant that we may all share together in the abundant goods God has given us and that we may help underprivileged countries.

AMEN.

Author unknown

A leader must have more of an armor of confidence in facing the unknown—more than those who accept his leadership. This is partly anticipation and preparation, but it is also a very firm belief that in the stress of real life situations one can compose oneself in a way that permits the creative process to operate.

Robert. K. Greenleaf, Servant Leadership

I beg you...to have patience with everything unresolved in your heart and to try to love the questions themselves as if they were locked rooms or books written in a very foreign language. Don't search for the answers, which could not be given to you now, because you would not be able to live them. And the point is, to live everything. Live the questions now.

Perhaps then, someday far in the future, you will gradually, without even noticing it, live your way into the answer.

Rainer Maria Rilke, Letters to a Young Poet

The best way to predict the future is to invent it.

Alan Kay, American computer scientist

I arise today
Through God's strength to pilot me;
God's might to uphold me,
God's wisdom to guide me,
God's eye to look before me,
God's ear to hear me,
God's word to speak for me,
God's hand to guard me,
God's way to lie before me,
God's shield to protect me,
God's hosts to save me
Afar and anear,
Alone or in a multitude.

Saint Patrick

The place God calls you to is the place where your deep gladness and the world's deep hunger meet.

Frederick Buechner, *Wishful Thinking*

Water flows from high in the mountains.
Water runs deep in the Earth.
Miraculously, water comes to us,
and sustains all life.

Thich Nhat Hanh, Buddhist monk

The language that God hears best is the silent language of love.

Saint John of the Cross

The best years of your life are the ones in which you decide your problems are your own.

You do not blame them on your mother, the ecology, or the president.

You realize that you control your own destiny.

Albert Ellis, psychologist and author

God's dream is that you and I and all of us will realize that we are family, that we are made for togetherness, for goodness, and for compassion.

Desmond Tutu, South African social activist

   The Unspoken Words

I note the obvious differences
in the human family.
Some of us are serious,
Some thrive on comedy.

Some declare their lives are lived
as true profundity,
and others claim they really live
the real reality.

The variety of our skin tones
can confuse, bemuse, delight,
brown and pink and beige and purple,
tan and blue and white.

I've sailed upon the seven seas
and stopped in every land,
I've seen the wonders of the world
not yet one common man.

I know ten thousand women
called Jane and Mary Jane,
but I've not seen any two
who really were the same.

Mirror twins are different
although their features jibe,
and lovers think quite different thoughts
while lying side by side.

We love and lose in China,
we weep on England's moors,
and laugh and moan in Guinea,
and thrive on Spanish shores.

We seek success in Finland,
are born and die in Maine.
In minor ways we differ,
in major we're the same.

I note the obvious differences
between each sort and type,
but we are more alike, my friends,
than we are unalike.

We are more alike, my friends,
than we are unalike.

We are more alike, my friends,
than we are unalike.

Maya Angelou, peot, author, civil rights activist

     The Unspoken Words

Laughter is the sun that drives winter from the human face.

Victor Hugo, poet

The love in my body and heart
For the earth's shadow and light
Has stayed over years.

With its cares and its hope it has thrown
A language of its own
Into blue skies.

It lives in my joys and glooms
In the spring night's buds and blooms
Like a Rakhi-band
On the Future's hand.

Rabindranath Tagore, The Jewel That is Best

Perfection is not attainable, but if we chase perfection we can catch excellence.

Vince Lombardi, American football player and coach

Bless all who worship you, almighty God,
from the rising of the sun to its setting:
from your goodness enrich us,
by your love inspire us,
by your Spirit guide us,
by your power protect us,
in your mercy receive us,
now and always.

The Irish Jesuits, Sacred Space for Lent 2017

Live simply so that others may simply live.

Author unknown

THE ROAD NOT TAKEN

Two roads diverged in a yellow wood,
And sorry I could not travel both
And be one traveler, long I stood
And looked down one as far as I could
To where it bent in the undergrowth;

Then took the other, as just as fair,
And having perhaps the better claim,
Because it was grassy and wanted wear;
Though as for that the passing there
Had worn them really about the same,

The Unspoken Words

And both that morning equally lay
In leaves no step had trodden black.
Oh, I kept the first for another day!
Yet knowing how way leads on to way,
I doubted if I should ever come back.

I shall be telling this with a sigh
Somewhere ages and ages hence:
Two roads diverged in a wood, and I—
I took the one less traveled by,
And that has made all the difference.

Robert Frost, poet

*A*lways remember that you are absolutely unique.

Just like everyone else.

Author unknown

NOTES

NOTES

NOTES

NOTES

The Unspoken Words

1928 U.S Book of Common Prayer, http://justus.anglican.org/resources/bcp/1928/BCP_1928.htm

A New Zealand Prayer Book: He Karakia Mihinare o Aotearoa. Collins, 1989.

Bonhoeffer, Dietrich. *The Cost of Discipleship.* SCM Press, 2015.

Brown, Brené. *The Gifts of Imperfection: Let Go of Who You Think You're Supposed to Be and Embrace Who You Are.* Hazelden Publishing, 2010.

Brown, Jackson, and Brown, H. Jackson, Jr. *Life's Little Instruction Book.* Thomas Nelson, 2012.

Buckingham, Marcus. *Find Your Strongest Life: What the Happiest and Most Successful Women Do Differently.* Thomas Nelson, 2009.

The Unspoken Words

Buechner, Frederick. *Wishful Thinking: A Theological ABC*. Harper & Row, 1973.

Coelho, Paulo. *The Alchemist*. HarperOne, 2014.

Craik, Dina Maria. *A Life for a Life: A Novel*. Carleton, 1865.

Fairless, Rev. Caroline Sproul. *What Does Love Require? A Family Violence Manual for the Church Community*.

Day, Dorothy. *On Pilgrimage*. Wm. B. Eerdmans Publishing Co., 1999

Foerster, L. Annie. *For Praying Out Loud: Interfaith Prayers for Public Occasions*. Skinner House Books, 2003.

Frank, Anne. *The Diary of a Young Girl*. General Press, 2017.

Gateley, Edwina. *A Mystical Heart: 52 Weeks in the Presence of God*. The Crossroad Publishing Company, 1998.

Greenleaf, Robert K. *Servant Leadership: A Journey Into the Nature of Legitimate Power and Greatness.* Paulist Press, 2012.

Hawkins, Pamela C. *The Awkward Season: Prayers for Lent.* Upper Room, 2009.

Hershey, Terry. *Sanctuary: Creating a Space for Grace in Your Life.* Loyola Press, 2015.

Hippo, Saint Augustine of. *The Confessions of St. Augustine.* Signet Classic, 2009.

Jones, Dennis Merritt. *The Art of Uncertainty: How to Live in the Mystery of Life and Love it.* TarcherPerigee, 2011.

Larson, Christian D. *The Optimist Creed and Other Inspirational Classics: Discover the Life-Changing Power of Gratitude and Optimism.* TarcherPerigee, 2012.

Levoy, Gregg. *Callings: Finding and Following an Authentic Life.* Harmony, 1998.

Lewis, C.S. *The Weight of Glory.* HarperOne, 2001.

     The Unspoken Words

Lindsey, Elizabeth. "Curating Humanity's Heritage." TEDTalks.

Loder, Ted. *Guerrillas of Grace.* Fortress Press, 2005.

Monson, Thomas S. "Finding Joy in the Journey." *The Church of Jesus Christ of Latter-Day Saints,* 2008, www.lds.org/liahona/2008/11/finding-joy-in-the-journey?lang=eng

Nouwen, Henri J.M. *Bread for the Journey: A Daybook of Wisdom and Faith.* HarperOne, 2006.

Pearce, Paula. *Prayers from Franciscan Hearts: Contemporary Reflections from Women and Men.* St. Anthony Messenger Press, 2007.

Pirsig, Robert M. *Zen and the Art of Motorcycle Maintenance: An Inquiry Into Values.* William Morrow Paperbacks, 2005.

Rilke, Rainer Maria. *Letters to a Young Poet.* W.W. Norton & Company, 1993.

Robinson, Marilynne. *Gilead: a novel.* Picador, 2006.

Tagore, Rabindranath. *The Jewel That is Best: Collected Brief Poems*. Penguin Books, 2011.

The Irish Jesuits. *Scared Space for Lent 2017*. Loyola Press, 2017.

Thompson, Vicky. *Journey to Spiritual Awakening: Meditations to Awaken the Divine Heart Within*. Journey with Spirit, 2002.

Tzu, Lao. *Tao Te Ching*.

Warren, Rick. *The Purpose Driven Life: What on Earth am I Here For?* Zondervan, 2012.

Wiesel, Elie. "Hope, Despair, and Memory." Nobel Lecture. The Nobel Peace Prize 1986.

Yeats, W.B. *Responsibilities and Other Poems*.

Danielle M. Gilbert has been a businesswoman and leader in the Richmond, Virginia community for over 15 years. Her passion for guiding the success and growth of others has led her into the role of entrepreneur, author, and speaker. *The Unspoken Words: Pain, Patience, and Progress* is her debut book.

To learn more about Gilbert and the services she offers, as well as the opportunity to buy her books or to hire her as a speaker for your next event, please visit: www.DanielleMGilbert.com

The Unspoken Words